W9-AHF-787

A NEW SET
OF EYES

OTHER BOOKS BY PAULA D'ARCY

Song for Sarah / A Mother's Journey through Grief and Beyond

Gift of the Red Bird / The Story of a Divine Encounter

When People Grieve / Guidance for Grievers and the Friends Who Care

Sacred Threshold / Crossing the Inner Barrier to a Deeper Love

Seeking with All My Heart / Encountering God's Presence Today

A NEW SET OF EYES

Encountering the Hidden God

Paula D'Arcy

A *Crossroad* Book
The Crossroad Publishing Company
New York

The Crossroad Publishing Company
www.CrossroadPublishing.com.

Copyright © 2002 by Paula D'Arcy.

All rights reserved. No part of this book may be reproduced, stored in a
retrieval system, or transmitted, in any form or by any means, electronic,
mechanical, photocopying, recording, or otherwise, without the written
permission of The Crossroad Publishing Company.

In continuation of our 200-year tradition of independent publishing,
The Crossroad Publishing Company proudly offers a variety of books
with strong, original voices and diverse perspectives. The viewpoints
expressed in our books are not necessarily those of The Crossroad
Publishing Company, any of its imprints or of its employees. No claims
are made or responsibility assumed for any health or other benefit.

Printed in the United States of America

The text of this book is set in 13/18 ITC Novarese.
The display faces are Linoscript and ITC Korinna.

Library of Congress Cataloging-in-Publication Data

D'Arcy, Paula, 1947–
    A new set of eyes : encountering the hidden God / Paula D'Arcy.
      p. cm.
    Includes bibliographical references.
    ISBN 0-8245-1930-2
    ISBN 10: 0-8245-2573-6 (pbk.)
    ISBN 13: 978-0-8245-2573-6 (pbk.)
    1. Meditations.   I. Title.
  BV4832.3 .D37 2002
  242 – dc21

                                 2002004437

2 3 4 5 6 7 8 9 10   15 14 13 12 11 10 09

No road is walked alone.
Sometimes love seems to come from nowhere...
undeserved and bestowed in armfuls.
To these friends who have immeasurably
brightened my path,
I dedicate these pages.

Randy and Ann Smith
Jack and Judi Holmes
Kim and Leslie Wheless
Hank and Kathryn Coleman

Contents

Private Roads: High Timber

This road takes you through high timber.

It flows like a red dirt river
mindful only of terrain —
just where to bend,
how to climb.

Plain, and with good purpose
it lays a course
up and up the mountain
into the cold beyond the trees —

Unaware that its signature is witnessed
by blue-black Ravens
and Red-tailed Hawks

or that it leads a procession of ardent yellow leaves
luminous in celebration

like a thousand Chinese lanterns.

C. C. Barton

Questions
of the Heart

I watch as the sun's first color circles the horizon. I put down *Everything Belongs*, written by my friend Richard Rohr. I've been reading the questions he asks in the book's Foreword, questions acknowledging the barriers to change.

For a long while my eye continues to follow the changing movement of morning light. Richard is expressing what my heart knows too well: I resist my own awakening. I push hard against that for which I most deeply long. I sense, deep within, that there is more: more to know, more to experience, more reality than my careful definitions of

God. I intuit larger places, and a greater meaning to being "born again" than only the assent of the heart.

But when the invitation comes to step past comfortable conclusions, my usual response is not to run toward this newness, but instead, to be afraid. In fact, to cling even harder to the ideas that keep God a careful object of study, not a Subject who will totally change the way I experience my life.

To awaken is not about staying in the same place and seeing, from there, new vistas. Nor is it about having enlightened insights, or realizing new thoughts or ideas. It is to find myself in the new vista, looking back at my former life with an entirely new set of eyes. It is, literally, to be changed; the spirit within becomes my sight.

As the red sun now covers cedar branches and yucca plants on the hill to my east, I pick up a pen and begin writing down the questions that burn in my heart:

Do I dare start fresh and let God, not my coveted image of God, lead the way?

Do I have the courage to ask if all I believe is the fullest knowledge?

What might it cost to move from belief to sight?

And if some of what I've passionately held to be true is only the smallest glimpse of something infinitely greater, what would convince me?

How do we become unafraid to see what we already are?

Reconsidering Cherished Beliefs

In the early '70s, as part of my work as a counselor for a small community college, I was sent to a federally funded drug education program held at Yale University. Upon arriving, two hundred counselors and educators were led into an auditorium and were given a word problem that had a mathematical answer. Without benefit of paper or pencil we had to solve the problem and then stand with any others whose answer agreed with our own. Three groups formed.

The largest group, which I joined, thought the correct answer to the problem was 38. Approximately eighty-eight others believed the correct answer was 21. Two men decided the answer was 11.

The program organizers then left, promising to return in one or two hours. In their absence they wanted each group to convince everyone in the room that their answer was the right answer. It was an exercise in group dynamics and peer pressure. But even realizing that, which we eventually did (but not quickly!), did not make the exchanges any less heated.

In time the largest group grew larger, becoming a clear majority. When the leaders reappeared, the second group had shrunk to thirty-five and the two men who originally believed 11 was the correct answer had never changed their minds, but also never convinced anyone else to join them.

I remember the evening with a certain vividness. The correct answer was revealed to be 11.

For myself, I had never entertained that possibility, clearly and logically having concluded that two individuals could not accurately see what one hundred and ninety-eight did not.

Many beliefs (especially religious beliefs) are so widely established, and so long held, that it appears "unthinkable" to question them. Even to quietly ask yourself if you agree without reservation, or to wonder whether or not the belief really makes sense, is to set yourself apart. Reconsidering strong and cherished beliefs is a formidable step. Perhaps this is why we seldom question the largest things, or why Galileo was imprisoned.

"The last experience of God is frequently the greatest obstacle to the next experience of God [because] we make an absolute out of it."

I wonder if my own heart can be courageous. It's so much easier to embrace religion than it is to encounter God. In encountering God I can find no reassuring doctrine that predicts exactly what steps to take, and how things will unfold. There is only a growing awareness that the lens through which I view my life is small; that my cherished views are, perhaps, only echoes of what is true. I suspect I must set aside many things I have learned in order to look past the barrier of those first conclusions. One day these learnings may be handed back to me, with an added awareness of their deepest meaning. But there is no guarantee of that, as something deep within causes me to think beyond what I've held to be right. I feel as if I am standing naked and alone.

Belonging to God feels without precedent. If I alter my sight and follow God, not an image, I will be changed. Somehow I know that significant ties tethering me to head knowledge and popular conclusions will be torn away.

In the movie *Contact*, starring Jodie Foster, there is a powerful scene portraying the tremendous change that is felt when new awareness is first experienced within the human frame. In the movie, Foster's character is set to move through time and space in a specially designed space capsule. However, the viewer soon realizes that she has traveled nowhere but to *this* planet, Earth, whose mystery she is now beginning to glimpse for the first time. She finds herself looking from an entirely different

perspective at ordinary things she has never noticed before: trees, sky, water, light. Things she has
always looked at, but never known.

It is that way.

Waiting for the Dance

I was standing in the central square of a pueblo in Taos, New Mexico, waiting for the Native American Ceremonial Dance to begin. Even though I had driven a long way to experience this ritual, my mind was filled with impatient thoughts: When will the dancers arrive? How much longer do I have to wait?

I moved restlessly around the square observing other visitors. We all took turns glancing at watches and searching the horizon for signs of movement. I tried to stand still in one place, and instead shifted my weight from foot to foot, willing things to happen. Nothing.

An hour passed. Then two. I memorized the shape and texture of the stones at my feet and noticed the exact way the last rain had pushed small dunes of sand against a nearby log. I considered the errands I might be running if only I had not arrived so early. I tried hard not to sigh out loud and seem impolite. Finally, I sat down in the dirt.

I think it was a crow that suddenly flew past, causing me to look up. His flight broke my mind's litany of the time I was wasting. For the first time I really noticed the adobe dwellings surrounding the square. Standing on the flat roofs of every home were Native women and small children, each wrapped in colorful blankets and shawls. They too awaited the Dance, but it was the quality of their waiting that seized my attention. There was no restlessness, even in the children. They stood from a place within. I could see it. They emanated a quiet that said, without words, "Something is about to happen. To experience it fully, you must be present. You must be joined to it with your breath and being. Then you will no longer be an observer. You too will dance, even though you stand still. You *are* the Dance."

My eyes lingered on their faces, their stillness. Watching them, I slowed my own breathing. The anxious words in my head gave way to words from a deeper place. Words spoken without sound. I let myself be led by a different kind of knowing.

I brushed dirt from my jeans, and now I too stood up. "Something holds all life in being." The thought was as distinct as the sunlight streaming down. "The Dance is not an event." it said, "It is life. Your life." Like the women, I turned and faced east, observing the power of a simple day. I barely noticed when the drumming started. It no longer mattered. For me, the Ceremony had already begun.

I do not stand in pueblos often enough. I sit too often inside my home or office, occupied by screens. Computers. Televisions. Calculators. I rush to airports and to appointments, my day-planner forever full. Some days I don't pause until

I sleep. I do this knowing that a full schedule does not serve me well. Knowing that many of my days have been spent living among people and places I did not see. I've lived in the future, waiting for "someday." I've taken up residence in the past, unwilling to let go. I've sat surrounded by books, reading about someone else's life.

Seeking with Empty Hands

It feels safe in my small world of conclusions and ideas. The physical belongings that surround me do not begin to reflect the size and breadth of thoughts and certainties that clutter my inner world, and define my vision. At any moment God could be dancing in front of me and I might look up quickly and say, "Not now, I'm praying. Don't interrupt my devotional time." The barriers are that formidable.

I used to think there was a formula or a set
"way" to follow,

but the inner journey seems to have no one
course.

Only that hands must be empty,

Heart must be seeking.

Treasured conclusions must be set aside.

Beliefs are small in front of Divine brightness.

It doesn't matter what I hold to be true.

All that matters is what is.

Such emptiness the Spirit demands

Such childlike trust

Such wanting

There Is Only This Moment

It was just a moment. The crush of steel, the terrible screech of brakes. Shattered chips of glass in my long black hair. My husband slumped over the wheel, my daughter, Sarah, moaning.

I lay twisted, frozen in that slice of time. In that moment the world, for me, became so still. No breath I've drawn has been so deep, or quiet. The only sound was the moment, reaching out to touch my future with its wake.

I was young, my arms filled with dreams, my heart innocent and trusting. Then the reality that I alone had survived. Their lives were over. And my heart's vigil as that knowing cut through me, appearing to be powerful and consuming...a monster with tentacles wanting to choke off my life. A long passage of time as I tried to understand how that moment could wield so much power.

But the moment actually held no power. The moment could do nothing. It waited to see what I would meet it with. By my act, the moment would confine me, or free me. Against Spirit, the moment was impotent.

Finally a new moment, when I held my husband's empty bathrobe and asked, "What is lasting? What cannot be destroyed?"

The moment I knelt at a window and breathed my first prayer, "If *you* are real, come. Let me find you."

The moment when a stranger anonymously placed a booklet into an envelope and altered the course of my thinking...and so, my attention. A booklet expressing the difference between knowing "about" God, and *knowing* God. Until that moment, I hadn't seen the distinction.

The moment when an aging preacher looked into my grief-filled eyes and said, "You didn't lose your life's purpose, you lost the purpose you *wanted*. They're different."

The moment in a courtroom when I looked into the eyes of the drunk driver who'd set this chain of grief in motion, and recognized my own soul.

The moment when I realized there is no safety. No promises. There is only this moment, containing the universe. Embodying everything. There is nothing more powerful than what you already hold.

Will I Let in Love?

There are no road maps. There is only what is true, and the choices we make.

It was the bedroom closet where my husband's empty shirts hung in a solitary row. Someone else would wear them now. I reached to the first hanger, touching the shirt collar and sleeve. I was ready to drop it into the Salvation Army box at my feet. Filling the small space of the closet was the question: Would I let in love again?

A courtroom. The drunk driver who set this treachery in motion calmly answering questions posed by the state's attorney. His eyes. His actions. My new reality. Would I let in love again?

Sarah's empty room. Her soft stack of play clothes. Her stuffed toys. The hooked rug with the smiling faces of Mickey and Minnie. The nightlight. All the pieces that had made up our world. Would I let in love again?

The black, red, and yellow checked flannel shirt, a gift from my husband on our second Valentine's Day. A faint smile of memory across my heart. It had been a disappointment, on that day. I had dreamed of flowers, or something lacy. Then the following Valentine's Day, and he was no longer alive. That day I "saw" the shirt for the first time. Would I let in love again?

Slowly finding my way. No longer focusing on what did not happen in my life, and seeing what was there. Glimpsing the beauty in exactly what I'd been given. Seeing all things as gift, and no longer asking why some were brief. Asking instead, why I hadn't held them more gently, with more knowing.

Now watching the pattern and movement of life with wonder, letting it move within me. Beginning to understand that the appearance of things is not the final say. The final say is the Love that moves invisibly, more tenderly and intimately than I can grasp. A love which awakens all matter from its sleep. A Love by which we are held.

We Choose
What We'll Risk

There is no protection against adversity

There are no guarantees

What you have is your Self, made

in the image of something very great,

the Greatest thing.

You have your Self, and

the particular circumstances of your life.

What you create

is your measure of love.

What you create

is up to you.

We choose what we'll risk.

But only the freedom that drives the risk matters

What Do I Really Want?

My chosen room at the retreat center in Indiana was tiny. Kneeling on the small cot, I could lean through the window and touch a slanted roof that was the runway for two squirrels. The branches of tall oak trees created a springboard for the squirrels, and also provided me with a small canopy of shade. At night, moonlight filtering through the branches covered my pillow, and I slept soundly in its circle.

The first morning I sat by the window with a list:

Do I want love, or do I want to be happy?

Do I want to encounter reality, or discuss concepts?

Do I want to be challenged to confront my weaknesses, or do I want to be taken care of?

Do I want to know God, or do I want miracles?

Do I want to live, or do I want a fantasy, a dream of what life should be?

Do I want to learn, or do I want illusion?

Do I want God, or my image of God?

Do I want truth, or my beliefs about truth?

Do I want life, or my idea of what life should be?

Do I want to see more than I'm programmed to see?

At the bottom of the list was scribbled, "FAITH —
openness to truth, no matter where it leads." I
picked up my journal and added, "Ego does not
see Love. It is not open to Love's disguises. It sees
objects, and other egos. Only when you look from
a different place (spirit) do you see what's true."

I drew a careful list of things I was beginning
to understand were illusion. Then a smaller list, a
beginning, of things I knew to be true.

ILLUSIONS

The idea that the earth can be "owned"

God as only masculine

God as a harsh keeper of scores

Heaven as a distant destination

The earth as insignificant to our awakening

Dominance as true power

Head knowledge as proof of wisdom

The measurement of time

THINGS THAT ARE TRUE

Love	Wind
Fire	Sun
Water	Spirit

I wrote, "I have a million reasons why my life is infinitely safer not questioning what everyone around me accepts as correct. I have a million reasons to honor my illusions. My ego is deeply vested in creeds and formulas that safeguard the mind's authority. I am not in the habit of stepping out of boats because someone insists the water will hold me.

"I thought it would be different. I thought I would be sitting by a fire reading about how the first-century Jews were confronted with the narrowness and even error of many things they believed and held sacred. I did not expect to live their same experience."

For the rest of the day I thought about what it means to give God everything. That night I dreamt

I was in a large building. On the upper floors were many rooms with old pictures and paintings. Someone my spirit knew came to visit, and I was excited to show him these rooms containing everything I had collected in my past. He walked respectfully through the rooms with me and I felt delight.

For a moment I followed someone else to the lower floor. I was almost dancing. But I was called again to the rooms upstairs and told to stand still. The radiant stranger waved his arm and I looked. All the rooms with my pictures and treasures were now empty. Everything was cleaned away, washed with light.

When I awakened I knew there was a power and a passion pursuing me, and not the other way around. I had formerly agreed to a concept that separated humans from God. I had agreed to a concept that told me there was something to find, and truths to know. I had agreed to a concept that substituted religion for my nature's true longing. I had agreed that there were correct beliefs and singular paths. I had agreed that I was my personality and my heritage, rather than a truer self outside that form, watching and observing. I had agreed that outer authorities and words were definitive, and that there was a God who was only pleased if I belonged to the right church and believed the agreed-upon creeds.

Now, I was in a boat, looking at the water, understanding that I must step out in order to be born again and taught anew, this time by Spirit.

What Am I Willing to See?

How much of my life will I spend being afraid?

What does it mean not to walk away when something no longer nourishes me?

What is it like to see, not what things look like, but what they *are* like?

Canticle of Love

Somewhere in our history religion became synonymous with God.

Religion is a longing *for* something, but it is not the thing itself. The thing itself does not need religion. In fact, religion may be a great barrier, because it is so rule-bound and convincing, so driven by ego. ("Our" God is the "true" God.)

Spirit, the thing itself, needs nothing to
    define it.

It cannot be described; it cannot be owned.

It can only be experienced in its wild passion
and its Love.

It can be encountered, not studied.

The mind cannot grasp it, though it will
forever try.

The way in is the heart.

That which we long for has the character of a
single relationship, with infinite forms.

All longing is spirit longing for itself.

Spirit may appear as a child, a starlit night,
new love, music, art, terror, tragedy,
beauty...

It comes disguised.

Seeing with New Eyes

This morning's drive to Santa Elena Canyon in Big Bend defies all desire to retell it with words. Over and over again my mind told me I was looking "at" something of great beauty, and I watched that thought take shape and persist. I followed it in the same way my eyes were following the passing monuments of stone, their rock faces fiery with early sun, and in the same way I was watching the birds fly with abandon. And a knowing arose that what appeared to be "outside" of me truly existed deep within. There *was* no separation. I was only watching a reflection.

This same morning my friend Maureen and I saw an ostrich, swallows, ravens, jackrabbits and cottontails. At one point the cottontails filled the road. River willows were ablaze with orchid-like blossoms. I heard the faint ring of the earth's vibrations, and had the experience of floating out of time, as if an inner part of me were soaring above those hills, free to go anywhere it wanted to be.

Arriving at the mouth of the canyon, we climbed cement steps in order to reach the river's edge and work our way through willows and reeds to reach the sand. Even in early morning, the heat was punishing. Where the mouth of the canyon opens, buzzards flew overhead. The wind in their wings, just inches above our heads, was loud and startling, like rawhide being whipped through the air. A yellow-bellied songbird performed from the top branch of a willow tree. Every vista became a feast.

Looking in each direction I had the sensation of watching a silent film. I consciously tried to match my breathing to the earth's, but found that I didn't know how. It was clear that Spirit commands everything, and whether or not we are aware of it, we live in Her embrace. Every other conclusion is created by ego.

Later that day, as I was hiking alone from our campsite, a jackrabbit hopped in front of me. When we were only three feet apart I knelt down to consider him from a closer perspective. He stared at me as I noted the surprising length of his legs, his tall ears. His eyes were brown, like mine. Eventually I began to walk away, but something compelled me to turn back to the rabbit a second time. Ever so slightly he moved, edging to his right until he was behind the gray, dried branches of a bush by the side of the road. He only moved five or six inches, but in that move he blended himself so perfectly with the branches that to my eyes he became momentarily invisible. I stared and squinted, and only with great difficulty could I finally distinguish the outline of his body from the lines of the bush.

"Fine job," I murmured appreciatively. "Amazing."

It *was* amazing. A small rabbit had just shown me how something may be present, but not be obvious at all. You have to look with a different set of eyes if you want to see beyond the ordinary.

Watching from a Distance

Her name was Robin, and she wore tights covered with wildly colored flowers and a T-shirt of lime green. She was barefoot, with long dirty blond hair pulled back into a loose ponytail, and I guessed her to be about seven years old. I had snuck into a church at an early hour, seeking a shaded, quiet sanctuary before beginning my intended day on one of the crowded beaches on Rhode Island's Block Island. Robin was standing impatiently at the doorstep. I slipped inside and found a pew where I wouldn't be disturbed. Several others sat scattered about, lost in private thoughts or prayers.

45

At the back of the church an authoritative priest suddenly announced that a girl named Robin was about to dance for all who were present. His body, in front of the only exit door, assured Robin an audience. I looked up without enthusiasm, and even some irritation. But Robin and her mother were already walking to the front of the church, a portable boom box in the mother's hand. When the box was plugged in and the "play" button pressed, Bette Midler's voice began filling the room with the Nancy Griffith hit "From a Distance." And Robin began to move.

It was immediately apparent that she was not entertaining us because of any unusual talent. It was a childish performance with awkward leaps and clumsy landings. Back and forth Robin flew, darting at first dangerously close to altar candles and then to statues of long-perished saints. But she was oblivious. Her attention was fixed on an inward place, her silky hair flying. She danced for love of dancing. She danced because she danced.

By verse two of the song a curious thing had begun to occur. Many in the church began sitting forward, watching more intently. By the second repetition of the chorus, we were all paying close attention. Robin's dance had come to get our hearts, and won. In that moment I knew my impulsive decision to find a quiet space that morning was telling me something more important than anything else I'd listened to that summer.

If we had any suspicion about who we really are, we'd be watching "from a distance" as the small story of our own life unfolds. We'd observe the roles we've adopted, and the temporary waves of thought and emotion that continually pass through us, but do not originate in us at all... thoughts and emotions common to every human being.

We are not the body and its functions. Amazingly, we are not dependent on the body at all. (One would assume death would have strongly taught us this, but we must not want to know.) We are the reality that stands behind the body. An inner being. And the body exists *for* this inner being. The body is the tool or vehicle that is able to move through time.

I once asked women attending a retreat to step forward, row by row, and "be seen" by those who remained seated. Connie, suffering with cerebral palsy, was furious and humiliated by my invitation, and raging with shame. She participated, but a lifetime of hiding had been violated and she felt angry and exposed. All afternoon she wrestled in private with the view of herself she had clung to for forty-four years. And somewhere inside the agony, which she heroically confronted head on, she stumbled upon the truth: I am not this body.

The next morning she entered our meeting room and asked me for the microphone, walking awkwardly but with determination to the front of the room. Yesterday she was protected by a line of others; this time she was alone. "Look at me," she said, tears streaming down her face. "Look."

"I have discovered what I am not. I am not these twisted limbs. I am not my inability to read. This is not who I am. I am the one who watches her. I am actually beautiful."

The first thing that must change is that in me which insists upon the smaller view of myself and tries to make that permanent. I must stand and watch from a distance, in order to discover what I am not. I watch my personality from the reality behind it. In that moment I am no longer identified with ego. Spirit begins to emerge and know itself. The dance changes.

I no longer dance to become worthy or prove my value. I do not dance to measure up or earn that which has belonged to me all along. I dance because I dance.

We risk the life we have known to discover something new...The unknown territory will open before us only to the extent that we turn our whole being courageously toward it...And then we must venture wherever the road leads us, in spite of the dark, in spite of the quivering of our heart.   — Jack Kornfield

It is the intensity of the longing that does all the work.   — Kabir

Seeing What's Hidden

In 1995 I traveled cross-country with my daughter, Beth. Late one night, in the small town of Galisteo, New Mexico, we stayed in an inn that sat like a jewel at the end of a very unlikely dirt road. We had driven miles out of our way to search for it. We almost gave up. In fact, if we'd seen other possible places nearby where we could spend the night, we might have. But there were none. We persisted, and the car's high beams swept the darkness one more time, and we found what we were looking for.

The innkeepers had gone to sleep, but guests from Ireland showed us to our room and encouraged us to watch the stars from the heated hot tub in the courtyard before sinking into our beds. The décor of the inn was bright and inviting. Every wall and corner were decorated and designed in southwestern colors and tiles, with flowers and plants in rich profusion. It was a welcome sanctuary at the end of a long day, and in the "home stretch" of our month-long trip.

The next morning, seeing things in daylight, we grinned a bit that the landmarks and turns had seemed so elusive the night before. We feasted in the inn's restaurant, which should have been six stars, if the ratings went that high. The brief hours spent in these surroundings renewed us for the hours of driving that lay ahead.

In the winter of 2000, almost five years later, I returned to New Mexico for a speaking engagement. While there I promised Kaye, the friend with whom I was traveling, that I would take her to Galisteo and a treasured inn I remembered fondly.

Leaving Albuquerque, we took a scenic dirt highway that led all the way to the little town of Galisteo, encouraged to do so by locals who promised us the ride would be worth the extra time spent. Alas, we had a long (and time consuming) ride on the "wrong" dirt road before finally finding the right roadway. Then we were richly rewarded by a first-class New Mexico sunset with its colors of mesmerizing beauty. We watched the shades of crimson and mauve blend to golden orange without speaking a word. For that brief moment nothing else seemed to exist.

But our lateness in getting onto the correct road also delayed us by many hours. And as the sun disappeared behind the hills, I realized that for a second time I would be driving to the Galisteo Inn in the dark. I still felt unruffled. I had been there before. I knew exactly what to look for. I excitedly described to Kaye how an old stone church would appear on our right. The church was our cue to make an immediate left-hand turn onto an unlikely dirt road. That road led to the inn.

We indeed saw the landmark church in the early evening. As we passed by I admired it and we spoke about the age and beauty of the stone. But since we were approaching Galisteo by a road that was new to me, the church came into our sight on a different side of the road; the opposite side from my memory. Since it was not where I was looking for it, and not where I was very certain it would appear, I never considered it might be the church we needed to find. After admiring its beauty, we drove on.

We traveled so far beyond Galisteo that I knew we had missed our turn. But we kept circling and searching, peering into the dark night for a church and a small dirt road. I stayed true to my belief that the landscape would appear in a particular way, but eventually we ran out of road and patience. We turned around and began to backtrack slowly. Arriving at the same stone church for the second time that night, I stared at it, comparing it to the image on the brochure I had sheepishly dug out of the pocket of the car door. I let my eyes find the infamous dirt road, which lay directly opposite the church when approaching it from this direction.

The truth was that two hours earlier I had already seen what I was searching for. But since it didn't agree with my image of it, I hadn't seen it at all. The image had become much more compelling than my sight. We spent precious hours looking for what was right in front of us. And I stared at what I was looking for with no recognition.

This is why "seeing" is so painfully elusive, and why we become blind to what is real. Our beliefs create images beyond which we cannot see, and our expectations obscure what we are looking at directly. In just this way we miss God, having already decided what we are looking for and how the Divine will appear. And we never find the road to the inn, even though we stand on it for a lifetime.

A Father's Tears of Love

It was Sunday afternoon and I was visiting my aging father. The cumulative effects of several years of strokes and surgeries had weakened him. Once a powerful lawyer who took care of things dogmatically, now he often cried with emotion, unable to believe his life had changed so dramatically. Physical limitations were forcing him to experience a powerlessness that felt frightening.

My father had been a difficult man to know. He was often lost in a silent place none of us seemed able to access. I knew so little about him. He revealed so little. And some of my strongest memories, regretfully, had been of the hardest times. Particularly the day in August 1975, when I lay in a hospital following the accident that claimed the lives of my husband and daughter. I was three months pregnant and fragile, and the morning I was told that my twenty-one-month-old daughter, Sarah, had just lost her life, I needed my father desperately. But instead of coming to my side, as did my mother, sisters, and friends, my father left the city where I lay shattered without ever visiting me and returned to his home in Massachusetts. He only reappeared ten days later, when the hospital released me to attend the double burial.

I could see no earthly reason why he didn't come to comfort me that day, and the pain of his absence had intensified a grief that was already more than my heart could bear.

On this particular Sunday my father and I sat at the kitchen table. Years had passed since my losses, and I had come to accept the mysteries of life, including who my father was and why he didn't care enough to comfort me. A series of strokes had now left him unable to speak for some time, so as my mother prepared a meal, I sat with my father asking questions that required only a nod or shake of the head. Characteristically, he still fought to shape words, even though that effort had been futile for a long while. Yet suddenly, in response to a new inquiry, a clear "yes" emerged from his throat. We were both startled. I made another remark and with great effort my father responded with a phrase. Neither of us had any idea why speech was suddenly possible, but I slowly began to ask more questions.

"What was the happiest time of your life, Daddy? What's your favorite song?"

To each question my father responded willingly, with increasingly intelligible words. The moment held such power that I decided to ask questions that would tell me things I had always longed to know.

"What was the hardest time of your life?" I asked. "If you had your life to live over, what would you change?"

For two hours my father revealed himself, and with his permission I wrote his answers down. I learned that he had never liked the practice of law, which consumed his hours. He had done it to provide well for his family. His heart longed to pursue a career in music. The irony was piercing. I'd hated his law practice and the time it demanded. Now I saw that it had been his measure of love. He had hated it too.

Finally he looked at me and said, "Sometimes, now, I want to give up." He laid his head on the table and began to weep. I went to him and held my arms around his shoulders.

"Daddy," I said, "you're exhausted. Let's stop."

"No," he replied, "I have to keep going. I have to tell you about the day Sarah died."

I inhaled deeply and waited. I didn't even know if I had the courage to listen. His absence on that day had so increased my suffering. And I knew, I knew, there was no adequate excuse. I had a grown child of my own now. If Beth's husband

and child were dying, what could possibly keep me from her side?

My father began, "That morning — that morning I went first to the hospital where they had taken Sarah and Roy. When I saw my granddaughter, I knew she was going to die that day. I found her doctor and made him tell me the truth. 'She's going to die, isn't she?' I said. The doctor nodded. I told him I knew. She looked just like Peter did just before he died." (Peter was my brother who died at age fifteen.)

"I walked away and prepared to leave the hospital, intending to come to the medical center where I knew you were waiting. But by the time I got to the door, I couldn't stop crying. I got into my car. It was 10:30 a.m. I only had to drive across town, but I couldn't stop sobbing and I couldn't find my way. I drove up and down streets, asking policemen for directions. But when I'd drive away I couldn't remember. I drove for eight hours, asking for help, getting lost, crying. Eventually I saw that I was in my own driveway, back in Massachusetts.

I don't remember getting there. I was attorney for the town at that time and I recalled that there was a town meeting that night. I went inside the house, washed my face, put on a suit, and went to the meeting. I never told anyone that something was wrong. I have never talked about this day until now.

"That day, when I was crying, I thought to myself, maybe now Peter and Sarah are together. So you ask me what I'd change about my life? I'd change their deaths. I would never have them die."

My father continued to weep, but after pouring out his long-held story, no further sounds were ever clear. His speech returned only for those hours. He died, two years later, still in a cocoon of silence. And I was left looking directly at the judgments I had held so righteously; realizing that what I had believed to be true was not at all what was. Yet I had believed it intensely.

"Argue for your limitations," writes Richard Bach in *Illusions*, "and they are yours." Or, as Russell Hoban says in *Turtle Diary*, "Prisons are all we know how to make." That afternoon I first began to understand what it might be like to look at what you have defined with certainty and see it with a new set of eyes.

And I wished, I so wished, that I might have provided this man with a greater experience of the love a father and daughter can know. I saw that these new eyes are not merely informed by wider vision and understanding. These new eyes are love.

Am I Willing to Change?

Hunt, Texas. My toe makes circles in the river, disturbing the water underneath the weathered dock. Immediate ripples move out across the wet surface, swelling in size until they reach the opposite bank, where a girls' camp is noisily in session.

Creation is always moving.

Shafts of light stretch across the cosmos; the same light that moves in waves throughout our cells.

My toe again unsettles the water.

Creation is still happening, still unfolding.

Moving.

Am I willing to unfold? To still happen? To change? To think past where my thoughts have ever taken me before?

Thomas Merton writes that we have "a mysterious inner alienation about being who we really are."

He goes on, "There is a hidden inner person, a living reality made in the image and likeness of God. . . . The secret voice of God calls us to take a risk . . . to consent to God's creative love.

"We come into the world born in a mask, looking as if we were only that person born of our mother. This appears to be the reality to which everything else in the universe is ordered. We spend life hours in this story. Only when my inner being emerges am I identified with God. But there is no rational way to arrive at this. Only God can teach me to find God. God looks at us, and a new being is born."

Unless the inner being emerges, our most secret drives remain unknown to us. We never suspect that there is a constantly moving inner scenery, with emotions coming through us from another reality.

Love comes from this unseen level. And fear, as well.

In truth, there is nothing that is really "mine," although I might say "my anger" or "my fear." "My possessions." "My money." These feelings flow through me, creating ripples, like the water. But all the feelings and emotions I know are known and shared by everyone else in varying degrees. And all that I touch exists because of a reality far different from the one I perceive.

Something else is present in us, and it comprises our true nature. Something else is in charge.

Knowing to Whom the Earth Belongs

I saw the sign in the distance, but seaweed and salt air had created a black film over its lettering. I was underneath it, looking up, before I could make out the words "PRIVATE PROPERTY." The meaning was clear: Do not walk here above the mean high tide line. No trespassing. We have a deed. The beach, the rocks are ours.

I stood stationary for a long while. The large marbled rocks on which this sign was standing have been earth beneath my feet for nearly twenty years. I have soothed my back on their warm surface and watched countless sunsets from their peak. Turning in the opposite direction, these rocks and I have honored the dawn.

I have sat crouched for hours in their jutting arms, writing, or simply watching the water from a cave-like nook. When my daughter Beth was young she poked for hours in their crevices, watching the snails attached to veins in the rock pools. Sometimes she returned home with snails floating in a green bucket of seawater.

As we sat on these slippery slopes, water washed over our legs during the hottest summer noontimes. On these rocks I grieved and learned to live again after the death of my husband and first child. From these friends I could look across the bay to Long Island Sound, many years later, when Beth moved to Manhattan to pursue a career in theater and film.

Walking underneath the sign, I slowly made my way over the rocks' aged faces, putting my feet down tenderly. I had been away for a year and there were many sentiments to exchange. The tide was low, and gulls and perhaps a dozen swans picked their way across the sand bar, hunting for breakfast.

These great stones are the sole access to a long stretch of remote beach that lies on their far side. The sand is silkier there, the beach strewn with seaweed and weathered tree trunks, perfect for sitting or leaning against while watching the water. I walked toward that beach, careful to keep my sneakers within the line of the mean tide.

When the first astronauts were hurtled past our atmosphere's gravitational reach, their eyes beheld humankind's first vision of the earth spinning in outer space. Color was what they saw. A pulsing blue white light. This was the glimpse they had as they were propelled through utter darkness.

As they watched the earth that momentous day, it is difficult to imagine that ownership and property boundaries made much sense to them, or occurred to them at all. At least, it is my deepest prayer that they did not.

I don't think they thought about dividing up the firmament, or killing others to own a speck of ground. My heart hopes they clearly saw one earth, and understood it to be alive. I hope they recognized the ego's folly and were humbled by all we do not see.

I know we will continue to erect signs. It will be inevitable until we experience our true nature, and until we look for guidance from within, not from without. I know the few voices that speak what is true will be largely dismissed, or not heard at all. I know human beings will calculate property lines and negotiate the ownership of oceans and even air. It may always be so.

I also know that the marbled rocks belong to no one.

Searching for Home

It was a time when I was struggling to live in the city, longing instead to settle near the ocean or the mountains where the natural world was more immediate. I needed my outer environment to more truly reflect my inner landscape. I suppose I was searching for home.

Sensing my unrest, a friend introduced me to someone she deeply admired, saying that he had deep knowing about many things. Hoping he might offer wise counsel, I found myself telling him about every painful trial I'd faced. The mountains I had scaled. Tears I had cried. Heartbreaks I had endured. I recounted my past in detail and held it up for his review. Here. Here is my suffering. My life. Here it is.

He sat in silence with me for long moments, his eyes surveying my face. It was difficult to guess his age. There was both gentle kindness and distance in his manner, and something else I could not identify at the time. A certain caring, perhaps, not about my pain and loss, but about whether or not, in this lifetime, I might get anywhere at all. Whether or not I might have even a single moment of awareness.

His response to my outpouring, when he finally addressed me, was just two words.

"So what?"

It's funny how things will happen. I could so easily have felt offended, except the love which filled his eyes changed the equation. "So what," plus the love, became a remarkable calling forth. As if he'd whispered, "Don't get lost there. It's not who you are. Those are experiences you've had. That's all. You're the self who lived through them. Know her."

I must have been ready.

I understood.

Alone in the Dark?

My friend Macrina and I arose early. After packing fruit and sandwiches into backpacks, we drove in semi-silence to the Arkansas forest where we'd planned to spend the day. It was fall, and four inches of multicolored leaves crunched beneath our boots as we walked from the car to the trailhead.

The cave we were looking for in this forest was set back about a mile onto our path, just as friends had described it. We surveyed its opening critically. I'd assumed we would be able to enter easily, through a wide opening, and be able to walk in half-light for a while before meeting the interior darkness with our flashlight beams.

But instead of a generous opening there was a narrow entry and pools of mud and rain water through which we'd have to wiggle our way to the interior. And then, what else might we meet?

In the end, Macrina demurred, the possibility of snakes feeling too likely. I decided to give it a try, if only briefly. With difficulty I wedged my body through the first window in the rock, hoping I'd be able to maneuver in exactly the same way upon returning. Light and sounds from the forest quickly dimmed, and there was only a faint echo within the cave to follow. I crept on hands and knees, following the sound. Past the first turn I could identify the sound as water. A few feet more, and there in the darkness was the full rush of an inner spring, a waterfall of cascading rain.

It is like that ... like a knowledge hidden deep within.

It's like being alone in the dark and then being aware that you are not alone. Something has revealed itself. You yourself can do nothing to make this happen. Thomas Merton writes, "...I cannot know Him unless He shows Himself to me..."

Deep within your own self lies a waterfall, a passageway to all other things. And you have a growing sense that the mystery of this passage is perfectly hidden and perfectly revealed in everything.

The Way Beyond Pain

Women representing nations around the world were attending a ten-day forum in Barcelona, Spain. On this particular day, two other women and I were briefly interviewed before the entire group in order to acquaint them with our areas of expertise. Then each woman attending was free to choose the topic of most importance to her and move to a separate room for discussion and reflection.

I was unprepared for my room to fill so immediately. I had spoken about the transformation of pain, and the women came steadily, requiring extra chairs to be found. In the first moments they began to tell their stories, asking with great sincerity how to find a way past heartache and sorrow.

I have participated in this same conversation in prisons, women's shelters, colleges and universities, church parlors. I have seen the human experience of pain, and the hunger to find a way beyond it.

The path is always the same. It begins with a knowing that the power is not in the circumstances I face, but in what I meet them with. It is my response to what happens to me that determines the course of my life. Pain is transformed when met with the nature that lies within; when met with that which is greater than pain.

This inner spirit is who I really am. My body is alive in this nature, and exists in its frame.

I do not need to be spiritual to find this. I only need to stop believing that the ego, the small self, is me. If I do, a different knowing emerges which has a largeness and a certain beauty. It is an expression of power and love beyond the usual definitions. To live in its knowledge is to know yourself to be free.

I watched that knowledge once in the face of

a young woman from Haiti. Sheraz. In her city at that time, electricity was available for only five to six hours per day, water much less frequently. At night it was not safe to leave your dwelling after 6 p.m. The streets were violent and the threat of harm continuous.

But when I hugged Sheraz goodbye, whispering "Be safe," into her ear, she stood back and looked straight into my eyes with her dark beauty. "Safe," she repeated. "It used to be my prayer. But now I recognize that we may not be safe. And if this is our portion, so be it." No sentimentality. No smallness. Only clarity. Power. Freedom. A beauty beyond the usual definition. The Self we most deeply are.

Circle of Beauty

The beach appeals to me the most in fall and spring when only the locals walk the shoreline. I like to roam before first light, hunting for hidden treasures. Sometimes I climb the marbled rocks to watch gulls search the water for crabs or shiny minnows.

On this particular morning I looked into a rock crevice and something bright caught my eye. I pulled until I was holding a discarded candy wrapper, ignorantly stuffed into that space. And there were others. I walked back to my cottage and returned with a large green trash bag. There was only one thought in my heart.

I knelt down and reached deeper into the crevice.

My fingers found hundreds of butts from discarded cigarettes. The stench turned my stomach. Wrappers. Bottles. Jack Daniels. Beer. Soda cans. Hidden in nearby grasses I uncovered rubber gloves. Dirty diapers. Six-pack cartons. Condoms. Paper cups. White plastic jugs. What is wrong with us?

I fought back tears and had begun tossing the garbage into my bag when I heard the unmistakable beating of wings. It was a forceful vibration. Sitting back on my heels I watched as twenty-two pure white gulls soared above the shoreline and formed a circle just above my head. Their movement was an expression of sheer beauty. As I looked they continued to circle. Then in one movement, they dropped silently to the sand and stood motionless in a circle around me.

They knew.

I continued to collect trash and the gulls never moved. They watched. My first bag was full and I needed several more. "Please," I whispered, "don't leave." I raced back to my cottage, but there was no need for me to hurry. The gulls were still standing silently in their circle when I returned. It took two additional trips and six bags to clear an area twenty-five feet in diameter.

When I twisted the clasp on the last bag, the gulls rose effortlessly into the air in one movement and again circled above my head with their white beauty. They formed a luminous hoop against the sky. Then in a single motion they flew far out over the water.

By then the sun had risen and its red light danced on the waves. I didn't move. I observed the sun moving higher in the sky, falling indiscriminately on the sand, trash, and shells. On those rushing to work. On every caste in every society. On all humanity.

I let it cover me.

All things are of one pattern made; bird, beast and flower, song, form, space... [They] deceive us, seeming to be many things, And are but one.
— Ralph Waldo Emerson

The Face of God

Trees offer themselves to the day with such ease, branches spread like outstretched arms. Beneath this oak, spiders have spun webs that move in waves across the grass. I half close my eyes and watch these strands, strung like long necklaces. They reach from blade to blade, ground to tree, trunk to branch. The smallest thread contains the full glory.

The birds are aware. So too the dragonfly, and the dew.

Rising from the dirt at my feet, a single blade of green draws my attention. It has forced its way through tangles of dried leaves, sticks, and dirt. I think it will be an oak. It's the smallest shoot, yet it, too, perfectly holds the sun. A little shock of green brilliance.

The green seems to intensify as I watch.

For all I know, I am looking at the very face of God.

Words in the Night

❧

At 9 p.m. I leave the Great Hall, where our retreat group gathered, and step into the full brightness of the moon. The night beckons, "Come." The heavens are filled with light, and I decide I will not trade this sky for the ceiling above my bed. I run back to my room long enough to pull on a pair of jeans and reach for a jacket, more for mosquito protection than warmth. Even the night breeze is warm. South Texas in July.

My flashlight casts a small circle of light on the road, but the moon radiates twice its illumination so I drop it into my pocket, glad that it won't be necessary. I plan to hike to a favorite spot near Silver Creek, where I know I can be distant from campers and other night activities.

I make three false turns in the woods before I find the exact dirt footpath I'm searching for. Negotiating my way over rocks and down steep declines is challenging in the shadows. I slip many times in the loose dirt, but gradually get my footing and night vision.

Passing trees, I reach out and feel their rough bark, rubbing my cheek against one of them, a silent sentinel by the river. As I'm standing there, I hear the distant, soft strains of music being sung in the darkness. I make a fast arc with my flashlight and see a large group of campers joined in a circle. There is no way past them without disturbing them, so I creep to a nearby log and listen to the beauty of human voices. When their circle finally breaks apart, their singing is replaced by choruses of frogs and crickets. I abandon my original route and lie down on my back in the grass, looking up at the stars.

"Don't be afraid . . . "

The words are clear, distinct, though not audible.

"Don't be afraid . . . "

The words come forward like a living force, and I allow them to penetrate me and fall inside. I don't know why the words are there. I was only aware of loving the stars, not of being frightened. The stars are brilliant tonight, tiny glimmering suns. I watch them until my eyes grow heavy. Then, knowing the hour is very late, I begin to retrace my steps, nearing our meeting place of several hours ago. Everything is still and I wish, as I often do, that the experience of this night could be shared.

Suddenly I am startled by a pair of eyes, which meet mine in the dark, almost close enough to touch. I strain to see in the shadows of the cedar, and finally make out the outline of a deer. He is watching me, and now he steps forward. In a low voice, I tell him what I have just been told: "Don't be afraid."

The deer shifts a foot, but still holds his ground. I inch closer. I eye his sleek body and he continues to look at me. In his eye I recognize another searcher for beauty, another lover of the night. I feel an unexpected sense of peace.

The deer is more than he appears to be. Everything is.

The Sound of All That's True

The town in Lithuania where I am staying was founded in 1338. I walk paths that have known footsteps for six centuries. The home where I am hosted, belonging to Vytas and Valentina, is wonderfully cool, a breeze from the lake blowing through the windows of my small upstairs bedroom. I watch neighbors pass by on their bicycles, milk pails hanging from the handlebars. A woman sweeps her walk with a broom made of branches. I notice the scent of roses.

Yesterday Valentina made cottage cheese, and today she boils milk in a large kettle to make a harder cheese for spreading. Our dinner was leek soup filled with vegetables from the garden. It was so delicious I questioned in my mind whether or not it was a healing potion. It surely could be. It drained away the long hours of flight from Texas to Lithuania and fortified me.

I am staying with this family because their daughter, Vaida, was one of eleven teachers who spent two weeks in Texas a year ago. The teachers came to America to experience our country, to open their hearts, and grow . . . Now, at their invitation, I embrace their own beautiful land. My friend Aurelia and her daughter, Thea, have also come. In the evening Vytas and Valentina speak of their years under a communist regime, and of Vytas' experiences as a boy living in exile in Siberia. I am moved to tears as they describe August 1988, just before Lithuania was finally granted freedom. This tiny country joined Latvia and Estonia to form an unbroken chain of hands, which spanned five hundred miles. Vytas and Valentina walked many miles to take their place in the human chain. As the people stood in declaration of their freedom, helicopters dropped flowers to encourage them. They stood in solidarity for half a day.

Over a two-week period Aurelia and I reconnected with most of the teachers who were with us in America. The reunions were filled with emotion, each expression of friendship and love exceeding the language barriers that might divide us. We learned to speak to one another without words a summer ago.

Communism exacted a price. It bred a deep mistrust, both of self and others. I had read about it, but now I was experiencing its fruit. We traveled to other cities in Lithuania, and the mantle of distrust and fear was evident in the places of commerce. Returning to Balninkai, where Vytas and Valentina live, we anticipate the arrival of Grazina, another of the teachers. When Grazina returned to Lithuania from America the summer before, she dedicated her future time to creating opportunities for the children of Lithuania, passing on what she had experienced while in America. She came with twelve children to meet us, and the eagerness and willingness in the eyes of the children moved each of us.

Throughout our stay, Vaida and her parents insisted that before we left they would bring us to the Anyksciai Forest, where we would be given a wonderful gift. I could not imagine a gift any greater than what I was already experiencing. But on the appointed day we left for the forest, driving for hours through the woods, stopping frequently to appreciate the land or a place of historical importance to Lithuania. Vytas had me taste a piece of clover from which they had made soups while living in Siberia in order to keep alive. The clover, the first piece of grass I had ever eaten and swallowed, was surprisingly sweet. We had lunch near Alantos and continued on, finally arriving at the home of Vaida's godparents, Jonas and Janina. They were elderly and frail, but radiated warmth. I was particularly taken with Jonas. He wore a blue, orange, and white striped T-shirt, a soft tan sweater, and a completely incongruous black Harley-Davidson cap.

Although we had already driven for hours, we were now directed back into the car to drive a short distance to a stone church which Vytas' grandfather had helped build. We found a place to sit in the few wooden pews, and waited. Finally Jonas walked slowly to the back of the room and began to climb a ladder that leaned unsteadily against the side of a small choir loft. Once inside the loft, he spoke soft words in Lithuanian that Aurelia translated for me. He was apologizing for the poor condition of the organ he was about to play. Then it was quiet.

My eyes were shut and I was marveling at where I was, that I was in this small church in this distant land at all. I heard the first measures of music from the organ and was thinking how lovely it was to have this experience. Then a solo voice took over the room, filling everything with its power, and my next breath came with difficulty. I have never, anywhere, heard a human voice so pure, a sound so penetrating. It was outside of me, and then suddenly inside of me, tearing down resistances

I didn't even know I had. It had total command of the atmosphere, its love so piercing that everyone began to weep involuntarily. It was more beautiful a sound than I would have known how to imagine.

It took several moments for me to find the will to turn around, to discover who had entered the room, and what manner of person this young man could be who sang with a voice that was so Divine.

Nothing prepared me for what I saw. When I finally focused my eyes on the choir loft, I realized that the young voice was coming from eighty-three-year-old Jonas, who was singing the "Sanctus," by Beethoven, with a beauty that could not be explained. It was like the Soul of all life summoning each spirit who listened: Here! Here is the sound of all that is true. Hear the sound of the Love to which you belong.

We were all in the sway of strong feelings. I wanted the moment to never end, and Jonas to never stop singing. When he sang, I knew things that I normally do not understand, but I could put none of it into words.

As Jonas sang I watched Vytas' face; tears filled his eyes. He looked straight ahead and far away. In his look I saw Siberia, the cold war, and all of man's inhumanity to man. I watched as the mark of human suffering moved across his countenance. Yet I knew that the power within that noble voice exceeded both individual suffering and all pain . . . exceeded them with a love beyond any definition.

That afternoon I learned that Jonas had been sent to Siberia as a young man because of that voice. Because of the remarkable gift. Those who were educated, or distinguished by a unique talent, were sent to build roads and live in obscurity. The years passed. Now he was an elderly man, but the voice had never aged. Truly, it existed apart from any space and time. It could not be contained.

Hand of Love

Sunrise

Pink-orange light rims the water,

the moon is full in the southern sky.

I arch my neck to better watch a flight of
seagulls in their V-formation.

I notice the feel of sand and water between
my toes

Everything in the universe breathes for God.

It does not matter what name is given to this
Presence,

Creator/Creatress

It only matters that as the Mystery begins to
    unveil,

the soul is stirred to recognition.

Everything that accepts form and is born
    of matter has a physical nature for a
    short while.

But the Force compelling this Play is true
    forever.

If you would know this Love, question
    everything.

Before Long

Before long
will come the time
to hate or love even more
in absolute contempt of middle course.
Before long the night will give its last battle
and we will face our fear of healing.

Before long dawn and evidence will rise
day will turn into light and light will hurt.
Fire will eat up the night
under our tightly closed eyes.

Before long
will come the time
to hate or love even more.

Kettly Mars, Haiti

The Power of Stillness

One winter, as I drove with a friend from Boston to New Hampshire for a cross-country ski trip, we drove into an unanticipated storm. Driving became formidable, and ultimately our four-wheel drive jeep got stuck in snowdrifts on an unplowed road. We set out on foot, knowing we were only a short distance from the cabin toward which we'd been traveling. Just a mile, and there would be a warm fire and hot food.

But the effort required to carry baggage and food supplies through hip-deep snow proved daunting. I thought to myself glumly that it was a perfect metaphor for long periods of my life: trudging with my "stuff" against all odds, clutching everything considered to be essential, moving it from place to place. As I pulled it along, it weighed me down.

That night it was ten degrees and snow was falling at the rate of an inch an hour. My jeans were immediately wet, stinging my skin. The resistance we met walking into snowdrifts made any progress painstakingly slow. My fingers were frozen inside my mittens, but I needed them to clench the clothesline we were using as a poor makeshift pull for the clothes basket filled with our groceries. It was a useless system, but the best we could devise. Every twelve inches the basket sank into wet snow, and it took all my strength to continually yank it along. The fire, hot chocolate, and a good ending would not come for another three hours when all our gear, including several gallon jugs of water (the only water supply), were at last safely carried to our lodging.

Two hours into this adventure, still moving with no noticeable progress toward our shelter, my friend and I became separated in the snow. Alone, I suddenly stopped in the dark and fought back tears, looking hopelessly at the great holes my legs were creating in the snowdrifts. I was cold, frustrated, and tired. Falling snow now covered my jacket, my hat, and my hair. It covered the trees. Yet in that agonizing moment I suddenly became aware that the world of this forest was completely still.

At that moment something within the storm seemed to reach out to me and command, "Stop." Just "Stop." I fell back into the snowdrift, letting it hold me like a soft chair. I loosened my tight grip on the clothesline until the weight of the basket was released, and then, finally unencumbered, I began to listen.

The silence of the storm dominated everything. There are no words to describe a quiet so potent. I knew the snow was echoing a stillness that exists, hidden, in everything. I do not understand how I suddenly knew this, but the knowledge filled me. I saw that this stillness generates all life. And sitting there in the snow I wept at the profound sound and power of that silence. It was hard to witness its beauty, knowing I'd lived many years never suspecting it was even there.

Continuing to watch the storm, I began to see the falling flakes as yellow bursts of energy, as light. It was as if lightning bugs had replaced the snow, and as I looked at that light I saw that its total composition was Love. I was looking at Love. It had become palpable.

There I was, a speck of a human being standing in the midst of a reality I couldn't begin to define. But for that one moment, I was seeing clearly. In that moment I saw who I was, and how distant that reality was from laws, beliefs, opinions, or creeds. The knowledge that was moving me transcended everything I had learned up to that point. It was a line of demarcation between what I had formerly believed, and what I now could see.

It amused me to consider that anyone wandering by might have looked at me and felt quite certain that nothing at all was happening. "It's only a woman standing in the snow."

Sometimes "former things" break up into small

pieces and are forever lost. After that moment it became impossible to still embrace "believing." I didn't even want to. Why would I covet an idea when reality itself was bursting with beauty and power?

The way I had always thought about things became expendable that night. Even God, as I had imagined God, or "thought about" God. I would never again be satisfied with abstract thought when I had tasted the experience of that Presence. The difference could not be compared.

That night I suspended many cherished beliefs. The snow was alive.

Throughout my whole life, during every minute of it, the world has been gradually lighting up and blazing before my eyes until it has come to surround me, entirely lit up from within.

— Pierre Teilhard de Chardin

The Hidden God

Almost capriciously, to help a retreat group visualize what normally is not seen, I created a one-act play dramatizing a two-year period in my life. There were two characters, God and myself, but only the audience could see and hear God, or watch God move. I appeared as if giving a monologue, oblivious to any presence other than my own.

The audience listened to God's voice guiding and reassuring me . . . sometimes pleading with me, "Don't give up now. You're so close. This is where everyone gives up. One more step and you'll be free." They watched as God pushed books toward me when I browsed in bookstores. They witnessed God's Love calling me to awaken, and to let sorrow break me open so that I would see what I had not seen before. They watched a God without any narrowness, imparting his light in the form of passion, dreams, and tender love. They could see this God evoking the name of the true spirit living in my heart.

The play was accurate. There is a God who exists side by side with us, but remains unrecognized. A God who compels our soul to defy the darkness of pain, and who lends light and power to the affair we call life. This God creates the seed for faith and for our knowing of higher things. This God is the truth behind our smaller truths. Because of this hidden God, human beings know of the existence of the Greater Soul. This God is cause and purpose of our being.

In the play, as long as I denied this hidden Presence, I saw things in duality — saw God apart from creation and removed from my human life. Not until I finally let go of my ideas about God, and the ways in which I tried to appease him, did I recognize what was already true: my life had been a continuous encounter with the divine. There was nothing else to discover. Deep within my cells this hidden Joy had always lived.

Curtain of Sorrow

I longed for the day to be a simple walk taken by two friends, another of the many hikes we each loved. But it was neither a simple nor an ordinary meeting. Susan's beautiful son, Mark, had died just weeks before, killed in an accident on his way back to college. So we walked in a curtain of sorrow, my friend's countenance drawn and her eyes without their usual light.

About noontime we found our way around the rim of the hiking trail and descended a steep footpath Susan wanted to show me. At the bottom, pushing aside dense plant growth and flowering trees, we found our way to a small rock overlooking a mountain stream. Huddled in this canopy of green we listened to the sound of water and let the damp air give our bodies cool relief. As we sat there in secret, with barely enough room for both of us on the rock, I felt completely hidden away. For that moment, no one on earth knew where to find us.

Then in that deep, wondrous shade we heard a sound. Next, we saw a flutter of wings, and a red cardinal unerringly found its way to the edge of the very rock where we crouched. Red birds are always beautiful to me, but this bird's beauty seemed even greater because of the isolation of our spot and the poignancy of his arrival at this time of Susan's intense pain.

We looked at him and then at one another. The gift brought tears to both our eyes. As we watched I knew the bird was so much more than a winged creature. I knew the nature of that Love that follows us to the farthest places. I knew its power and passion, ever pushing from within us. Guiding. Calling forth. Only the form was a surprise. Everything else I recognized.

Giving My Freedom Away

It was a disturbing dream. In the dream, my brief life span has ended, and I am looking back at the character of my journey. Now that I am no longer immersed in the hours and days, I recognize that everything is astonishingly beautiful. Physically, the earth is wondrous. Why did I seldom look more closely?

Watching from afar I notice the moments as they come and go. I see the opportunities to become aware, and watch myself choose the safety of sleep. I observe the people who populated my small circle . . . the characters in my "story." I remember their seeming power, then, to validate and sometimes define me. I recall longing for their approval.

But it is clear to me from this perspective that they had no power at all. The only power they had was given to them by me. It seems an incredible irony. My freedom was never wrested from me. I handed it out in large and small pieces.

Now it's obvious that limiting "me" wasn't even their objective. They were only wrestling with their own need to feel worthwhile. A great sadness fills me. What if I had interacted with life in a different way? What if I had supported everyone I knew in the discovery of the truest things?

Why did I walk away from so many opportunities? Why were there corners and people I never explored?

My days were intended to be full of delight, but I took it all so seriously. I created a small nesting place, and decided that my tiny domain was the center of all that mattered.

I was angry when I should have laughed, and I

laughed when I should have cared. Over and over I felt trapped and imprisoned when I was just one choice away from being free. I leaned away from life, never learning how to lean in.

In the dream, it was too late to relive any moment. I was aware that I had seen some things clearly, but many things not at all.

I awakened, heart pounding, unable to recognize at first where I was. Slowly the room came into focus. I was stretched out on the floor of a loft, tangled in my sleeping bag. The windows were open and the sweetness of an ordinary morning awaited me. Except for the sound of a single bird, all was still. A deer grazed beneath the window. A squirrel scratched its way up a nearby tree.

I followed the line of morning light as it fell onto my sleeping place. I noticed a spider edging along my pillow, creeping toward me.

Here is the true task: to awaken from the dream and recognize that everything is alive.

The Heart's Cry

We make a difficult demand on life . . . that it
    be safe and secure.

We make a difficult demand on you . . . that
    you live up to our own beliefs about you.

It is not that way.

You take us in and breathe us out.

You refuse to gratify that which is not clear in
    our hearts.

You pursue when we hide in narrow places.

You are wide, limitless possibility,

the embodiment of every longing.

110

When we get anywhere close to your true
essence, we become frightened, because
it is too real.

Yet you refuse to remove our great darkness,
until we long for your light.

Even the elements obey you.

It will not be finished until we remember who
we are.

The Soul's Deepest Longing

I watch them float against the blue morning, these ribbons tied to tipi poles, stretching over the fabric that creates my desert home. Sunlight races with them as they fly, red markers of my dwelling. And I, who have visited cathedrals of renowned architecture and touched fabrics of elegance, let tears stream down my face at the beauty of the ribbons, their movement in the wind, their grace, all somehow a mirror of the streams of longing I feel in my own heart.

When I walk from camp in any direction I look back to see their passion flying. By them I mark my way. They are the heralds, doorways to mysteries I little glimpse. I think of the generations who lay down beneath such ribbons, dancing, celebrating, lovemaking, grieving . . . but always knowing that the earth beneath their feet was breathing.

Past midday I watch the reflection of their red fire in the shadows dancing on the sand. I can touch them, now, in illusion. Can trace my fingers along the line of their reflection. Can see them captive, momentarily, in the dirt.

Ribbons. I watch them as a thousand galaxies light the evening sky. I see them lifted to the wind, unresisting, dancing with abandon for the moon.

Lantern light from inside the center of my desert home rises to illumine the brightness of the ribbons in this nighttime revelry . . . their sweetest reflection of the spirit that moves through all things . . . that moves through me. I breathe in that reality, breathe it out, like prayer.

Covered by the peaceful night sky I walk softly down the path to a distant point where I stand for long moments in my place of worship. I am no one and I am everyone. I am pursued by a passionate love which will not let me go. No words fill my mind. No images. Only my breath as I breathe into the desert and let its beauty pour through my being. I raise my eyes and in the distance see yellow light from the tipi, my small haven against the darkness. The ribbons still stream atop its poles, reminders of what it means to simply be.

Paradise

Feel me in the sun, covering
you day after day . . .
I rise with color and glory, sustaining life.
I offer flowers and grasses,
trees and grains,
each form an expression of my One Being.
There is only one inventor,
One musician,
One poet,
One muse
All thoughts and emotions emanate from One Spirit
defined on earth by matter and form.
Your human eye looks at the vastness and
takes in nothing, without my willing it.
You want to keep me safe, as theory,
and shy from the true encounter.
You live in a garden you are not able to recognize
And in a Paradise that escapes your vision.
There is no great mystery.
Nothing to find, no important words to remember.
When you are finally ready
You will know.

The Problem of Pain

A few years after my first book, *Song for Sarah*, was published, I wrote a sequel called *Where the Wind Begins*. Although this sequel has been out of print for many years, I still receive requests and comments from those who particularly liked its format. A favorite section was the chapter where I "thought out loud" about the problem of pain, and wrestled with why suffering and evil exist.

In recent years I've thought again about evil, and suffering, and the meaning of life. After writing a play in which God is visible and speaks his thoughts about the purpose and value of life, I began considering what the devil might say if given a similar opportunity. But when I listened for those imagined words, what I heard surprised me. It was not what I expected a devil would say. Instead of a sinister tone, I heard:

Human being, I marvel that you deny what lives within you! At least I *am* my evil nature. But you? You are separated from your nature! The small, ego-self you take yourself to be is not you! And you do not see this. You cling to an identity that is only temporary and was always meant to be so. Why can't you see that the small self is only a means for the Spirit that exists beyond the surface?

I laugh that you will not transcend your limited sense of yourself. There have been rare souls that delighted the universe with their beauty. You could be like them. But you choose to stay lost in denial and blame, con-centrating your effort on saving and perfecting the mask you wear. You miss your life by staying in narrow places of fear. How tragic, because you are a vast soul, capable of never-ending passion. But you do not know this. Instead you believe you are separate from God. Because of this you never search for your truths in the one place you will find them, your own heart. God does not live in a far-away place, distant from you. That which you seek is already there.

And pain is not your enemy, nor am I! It's pain that breaks the structure of the mind and ego, producing the possibility that something else may emerge. Pain reveals to you the power of your illusions. The moment you meet pain with that which is greater, with the hidden joy and truth that lie within, there will no longer be a need for pain at all. When you rise up and meet the Divine in you, you will not experience powerlessness any more.

Believe me, I am not your problem. The problem is that you do not know who you are. And I shall exist for as long as you do not know.

Lead will play its role until the world has no further need for lead; and then lead will have to turn itself into gold.

— Paulo Coelho

Our Secret Nature

❦

To be born again isn't a belief.

It's a complete change.

Biologically we are the crown of life.

Mentally, we are quite apart from other creatures.

Emotionally, we experience feelings and responses that others do not.

But we are not yet fully developed, fully manifested spiritual beings.

Our actions are still pervaded by ego . . . by a sense of "I" and "mine."

And Spirit may be present in all its creations,
but we will not know this.

We see things to oppose, not embrace.

We live apart from the dictates of our true
nature.

We allow ourselves to become the servants
of our blind hearts.

We even institute ourselves as kings and
queens.

If it is true that humanity is the child of God,

then there is a secret nature to us.

All our beliefs and religions, all our theologies
and philosophies imply the presence of
another nature that is meant to be ours.

All spiritual teachings point to this in
some way.

There is a spiritual domain within us.

A power greater than our ordinary power.

An intelligence more keen and perfect in its understanding than our ordinary mentality.

A greater heart from which truer emotions can rise.

A true self, capable of exceeding the limits of our ego.

A Kingdom of God we must enter . . . that we must be able to be born into.

Our ego would like to believe we could remain just as we are, and assent to this nature mentally . . .

Do good works, and accomplish the deed.

But for Spirit to be born into our human nature, a great change must come about that encompasses all we perceive ourselves to be.

Jesus speaks of this possibility here on earth. But we do not dream of it here, in this world. We don't believe it's possible. We resist realizing that the Spirit can exist when and where we are. So the secret inner nature remains hidden and unrealized, confined to the "hereafter."

What if the soul we declare to be invisible, caged somewhere inside of us, is actually the thing that defines and contains us?

What if we do not make our soul more or less acceptable by our virtues or good deeds?

What if the soul has never been away from the heart of God?

What if the soul, the true child of God, labors so that our human nature can find its way back to being a true image of God on the earth?

What if the Spirit has the power to create and labor even under the limited conditions imposed by matter?

What if the Spirit continues this work, whether or not the human heart and mind can consider or accept it?

What if faith is the forerunner of true seeing ... is actually an act of seeing?

What if we had the desire — or courage — to find God where it counts the most, in life?

What if we knew that within our very cells is a God-given energy, a source of light that possesses the secret of God's beautiful and complex design?

What if we understood that from this hidden place (this secret nature) comes everything that is?

What if our hearts desired to know?

Private Roads:
Taos Morning

It was the road itself
that made me walk it.

A cut of smooth earth,
a corridor ~ opening
to the tall green rhythm of trees.

Walking into the alchemy
of the hot morning sun
and the cold crisp air,
I round the bend and disappear

into the very breath of God.

                                    C. C. Barton

Notes

Page 10: Richard Rohr, *Everything Belongs: The Gift of Contemplative Prayer* (New York: Crossroad, 1999), 11.

Page 15: "The last experience of God is frequently the greatest..." Rohr, *Everything Belongs*, 47.

Page 16: *Contact*, dir. Robert Zemeckis, perf. Jodie Foster, Warner Bros, 1997.

Page 50: Quotation from Jack Kornfield, *After the Ecstasy, the Laundry* (New York: Bantam: 2000), 45.

Page 50: Quotation from Kabir, as cited in Kornfield, *After the Ecstasy, the Laundry*, 45.

Page 61: "Argue for your limitations...." Richard Bach, *Illusions* (New York: Delacorte Press, 1977), 75.

Page 61: "Prisons are all we know how to make...." Russell Hoban, *Turtle Diary* (New York: Morrow/Avon, 1982), 20.

Page 64: "A mysterious inner alienation...and a new being is born." Adapted from Thomas Merton, *New Seeds of Contemplation* (New York: New Directions, 1961), 21–36.

Page 74: "I cannot know Him...." Thomas Merton, *Thoughts in Solitude* (New York: Farrar, Straus and Cudahy, 1956), 97.

Page 80: Emerson quotation from *America the Beautiful, in the Words of Ralph Waldo Emerson* (Country Beautiful Corporation, 1970), 11.

Page 101: Teilhard de Chardin, as quoted by Annie Dillard, *For the Time Being* (New York: Alfred Knopf, 1999), 13.

Page 119: Quotation from Coelho, *The Alchemist* (New York: HarperCollins, 1998), 133.

Acknowledgments

Special thanks to Roy M. Carlisle, an extraordinary editor. When my edited first draft arrived decorated with his green post-it notes, my heart sank. I turned the pages and felt only the weight of his questions and challenges, barely taking in the final words of praise. Slowly I learned that this was not a job for him; he intended to hold these words with me until each of them reflected the clearest expression of my spirit. Writing in such partnership changed the way my own eyes see, and was more gift than I know how to say.

I also acknowledge John Tintera, a marketing manager with great sensitivity.

My grateful thanks to: my daughter, Beth, who

was with me during the writing of these pages, and who so generously honored the silence I needed; to Carole Hovde, Judy Parker, Anne Williamson, Waynoka Lawrence, and Bea Brock, beautiful friends who supported my writing time with practical gifts of food and hearts filled with encouragement and love; to Kettly Mars, a radiant woman whose poetry speaks to the world; to Marcia Hodges, Judy Bentley, Meredith Price, Susanne Lambert, Sandra Locke-Godbey, Meg Hunter, and Jan Christopher, powerful women from Alabama who "take me away" for a week each year and re-create the meaning of friendship and play; to Susan Goldby and Pam Van Dyke, my sisters in every way, whose eyes are always eyes of love; to Maureen Mangen, Kaye Bernard, Edita Bartnikaite, Aurelia Palubeckas, Thea Stewart, Vaida Zlatkute, Macrina Wiederkehr, Connie Barrios, Sheraz Saint Lot, extraordinary women who traveled some of these roads with me and let me tell our stories; to Mary Cox, Kirby Hlavaty, Susan Oakley, and Madeline Tyng, so dear to my heart, so strong in their visions, whose encouragement surrounds me; to my friends in Lithuania, my friends in Haiti, the men and women in prison, all of whom have taught me much about new sight. Finally, my grateful thanks to C. C. Barton, poet and artist, creator of beauty, for her words and her spirit. (*www.ccbarton.com*)

About the Author

Paula D'Arcy, a writer, church retreat leader, and conference and seminar speaker, travels widely in the United States, Canada, and abroad. She is also President of the Red Bird Foundation, which supports the growth and spiritual development of those in need and furthers a ministry both to those in prison and those living in third world or disadvantaged cultures.

A licensed psychotherapist who has ministered to those facing issues of grief and loss, Paula worked with the Peale Foundation, founded by Dr. Norman Vincent Peale, from 1980 until his death in 1993. In recent years she has frequently teamed with Richard Rohr in presenting seminars on the Male/Female Journey. Her individual work includes leading women in Initiation and Rites of Passage.

Paula's ministry grew from personal tragedy. In 1975 she survived a drunk driving accident which took the lives of her husband and twenty-one-month-old daughter. Pregnant at the time, Paula survived the accident to give birth to a second daughter, Beth Starr, who currently pursues a career as a professional actress.

For more information, including a speaking itinerary, visit *www.redbirdfoundation.com*.

Of Related Interest

Paula D'Arcy
GIFT OF THE RED BIRD
A *Spiritual Encounter*

NOW IN PAPERBACK

When Paula D'Arcy lost her husband and baby in a car crash, she began an inner search for a faith that was stronger than fear. In *Gift of the Red Bird* she shares her remarkable spiritual adventure: Paula literally journeyed alone into the wilderness for three days, allowing the Creator to speak through that creation. As she surrendered to the power of God alone, a red bird appeared and, without words, began to teach . . .

0-8245-1956-6, paperback

Of Related Interest

Paula D'Arcy
WHEN PEOPLE GRIEVE
The Power of Love in the Midst of Pain

Since the publication of her first bestseller *Song for Sarah*, Paula D'Arcy has become an internationally renowned expert in grief and bereavement issues. Now in a completely revised and updated version of an earlier book, Paula helps us understand how to cope with the process of grief and also how to reach out to others in the pain of grief. This classic manual is full of practical advice.

0-8245-2339-3, paperback

Paula D'Arcy
SEEKING WITH ALL MY HEART
Encountering God's Presence Today

With her distinctive literary style and spiritual insights, Paula D'Arcy brings fresh air to our spiritual reading. Here, in short, meditative essays, she reflects on twenty-nine passages from Scripture and shows how they are powerful, unpredictable, and life-giving.

0-8245-2109-9, hardcover

Of Related Interest

Paula D'Arcy
SONG FOR SARAH
A Mother's Journey through Grief and Beyond

Words cannot express the anguish, the sorrow, and the vast emptiness we face when a loved one dies. Hope itself seems to pass away with the one we love. Yet it is in the midst of death that we find the truth that leads us back to life. In this collection of tender, loving letters, written before and after her daughter Sarah's death, Paula D'Arcy transforms her sorrow into a gift of love that offers peace, comfort, and true hope.

"Paula D'Arcy has given totally of herself in the writing of this journal . . . begun with such love and completed with such courage."

— Joan Walsh Anglund, author of
Prayer Is a Gentle Way of Being with God

"Thank you, Paula, for sharing with us your human heart and your unmovable God."

— Joni Eareckson Tada,
co-author of *When God Weeps*

978-0-8245-2523-1, paperback

Of Related Interest

Paula D'Arcy
SACRED THRESHOLD
Crossing the Inner Barrier to Deeper Love

In the midst of her own story of recovery from devastating life events, we journey with Paula D'Arcy as she seeks to counsel clients and relate to friends and family when conventional ways of relating are not good enough. The book features the story of Paula's work with Morrie Schwartz of *Tuesdays with Morrie* as well as the stories of her journey with Julia, a woman serving a prison sentence for drunk driving; Scott, a troubled young boy; and with her aging father. These powerful stories invite us to reconsider the nature of love and the thresholds we must cross in order to love honestly.

"Paula captures with clarity the mysterious desire of our hearts — to love outside the walls of convention, and experience love's miraculous transformation. A must read."

— Carmen Renee Berry, co-author of
New York Times bestseller *girlfriends*

0-8245-2465-9, paperback

Of Related Interest

Joyce Rupp
DEAR HEART, COME HOME
The Path of Midlife Spirituality

Joyce Rupp shares her own hidden midlife journey, its ups and downs, with such honesty and insight that readers will identify with and benefit from the discoveries she has made along the way.

0-8245-1556-0, paperback

Joyce Rupp
YOUR SORROW IS MY SORROW
Hope and Strength in Times of Suffering

Rupp relates the Seven Sorrows of Mary to our own sufferings and opens for us a vast reservoir of courage, strength, and wisdom.

0-8245-1566-8, paperback

Of Related Interest

Barbara Fiand
PRAYER AND THE QUEST FOR HEALING
Our Personal Transformation and Cosmic Responsibility

A fresh look at prayer that probes the unity of human-kind in its brokenness with the entire cosmos as it groans for redemption.

0-8245-1812-8, paperback

Ronald Rolheiser
THE SHATTERED LANTERN
Rediscovering a Felt Presence of God

Rolheiser teaches us that the way back to a lively faith "is not a question of finding the right answers, but of living a certain way. The existence of God, like the air we breathe, need not be proven..." This work shines new light on the contemplative path of Western Christianity and offers a dynamic way forward.

0-8245-1884-5, paperback

Of Related Interest

Henri Nouwen
THE ONLY NECESSARY THING
Living a Prayerful Life

Compiled and Edited by Wendy Greer

Prayer is the dominant theme of Nouwen's books, his talks, and his life. This rich, deeply inspiring book will surely become the authoritative edition of Nouwen's writings on prayer.

0-8245-1833-0, hardcover

Henri Nouwen
FINDING MY WAY HOME
Pathways to Life and the Spirit

A collection of four essays, three previously published by Crossroad and here revised, that examines four different aspects of our spiritual life: the Path of Waiting, the Path of Power, the Path of Peace, and the Path of Living and Dying (never before published in book form).

0-8245-1888-8, hardcover

Of Related Interest

Henri Nouwen
BEYOND THE MIRROR
Reflections on Death and Life

"This small work may be Henri Nouwen's most honest and insightful.... That is saying quite a bit when one considers the prolific output by the late spiritual writer." — *Critical Review Service*

Beyond the Mirror, about Nouwen's near-death experience in 1989, has been unavailable since 1997. This new edition includes a Foreword by Robert Durback and an Afterword from the Henri Nouwen Archives about preparing for death.

0-8245-1961-2; paperback

Henri Nouwen
HERE AND NOW
Living in the Spirit

In this book of meditations, Nouwen shows a personal and insightful way that God is much closer than we ordinarily realize.

0-8245-1967-1, paperback

Of Related Interest

Henri Nouwen
SABBATICAL JOURNEY
The Diary of His Final Year

Now in paperback!

"*Sabbatical Journey* is must reading for Nouwen fans and
a fine introduction to the man for the uninitiated . . .
This journal reveals much about the heart and mind of
a theologian who has touched the lives of millions . . . "
— *Commonweal*

0-8245-1878-0, paperback

William H. Shannon
SILENCE ON FIRE
The Prayer of Awareness

Shannon takes readers on a guided journey through
a kind of prayer that is built on faith and leads to
a unique but accessible way of coming to know God.
This book incorporates spiritual insights from the East
as well as the West.

0-8245-1848-9, paperback

Of Related Interest

Thomas Keating
REAWAKENINGS

Keating examines key events in the ministry of Jesus, the important parables that were recorded, and the many celebrations of his presence.

0-8245-1149-2, paperback

Thomas Keating
THE HEART OF THE WORLD
An Introduction to Contemplative Christianity

"...the reader's introduction to contemplative Christianity will result in his or her eternal friendship with it."   — *The Liguorian*

0-8245-0903-X, paperback

Check your local bookstore for availability.
To order directly from the publisher,
please call 1-800-888-4741 for Customer Service
or visit our website at *www.cpcbooks.com*.